High-Tech DIY Projects with 3D Printing

Maggie Murphy

PowerKiDS press.

New York

Published in 2015 by The Rosen Publishing Group, Inc.
29 East 21st Street, New York, NY 10010

First Edition

Editors: Jennifer Way and Jacob Seifert
Book Design: Andrew Povolny
Photo Research: Katie Stryker

Photo Credits: Cover Hiroshi Watanabe/Taxi/Getty Images; Cover, pp. 12, 13 Ultimaker; pp. 4, 8, 16, 17, 21 (bottom), 23 Bloomberg/Getty Images; pp. 5, 7, 27 Airwolf 3D; p. 6 Business Wire/Getty Images; pp. 9, 11, 14 © AP Images; p. 15 Purestock/Shutterstock.com; pp. 18 (top/bottom), 25 Katie Stryker; p. 19 Tannjuska/ iStock/Thinkstock; p. 20 Fuse/Getty Images; p. 21 (top) © iStockphoto.com/tomasmikulas; p. 22 George Doyle/ Stockbyte/Thinkstock; pp. 24–25 Autodesk Tinkercad; p. 26 © iStockphoto.com/Latsalomao.

Library of Congress Cataloging-in-Publication Data

Murphy, Maggie, author.
 High-tech DIY projects with 3D printing / by Maggie Murphy. — First edition.
     pages cm. — (Maker kids)
 Includes index.
 ISBN 978-1-4777-6670-5 (library binding) — ISBN 978-1-4777-6676-7 (pbk.) —
 ISBN 978-1-4777-6657-6 (6-pack)
 1. Three-dimensional printing–Juvenile literature. I. Title. II. Title: High-tech do-it-yourself projects with three-dimensional printing.
 TS171.8.M87 2015
 621.9'88—dc23
                           2014000723

Manufactured in the United States of America

CPSIA Compliance Information: Batch #WS14PK9: For Further Information contact Rosen Publishing, New York, New York at 1-800-237-9932

Contents

3D Printing Is Fun!

A 3D printer is a machine that lets you turn a **digital model** of something on a computer into a **three-dimensional** (3D) object that you can hold and use. These printers make all sorts of things, from toys to **replicas**, or copies, of ancient **artifacts** to spare parts for space stations.

This figurine was just printed on a 3D printer. Many people design and 3D print their own figurines.

⚠ WARNING
HOT SURFAC

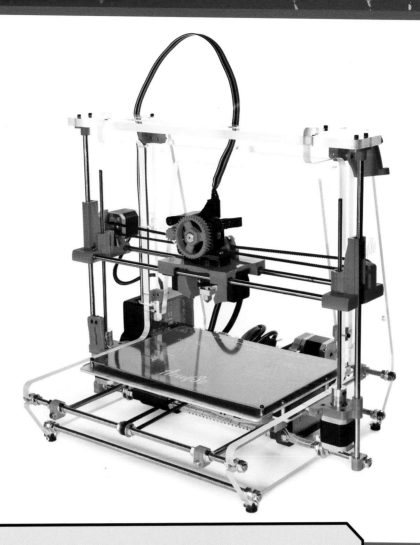

Home 3D printers, such as this one, are small enough to fit on a desk or table.

Kids all over the world are using 3D printers to make awesome projects like the ones you will find in this book! When you use a 3D printer, you are taking part in the maker movement. The maker movement is all about kids learning to do high-tech do-it-yourself (DIY) projects themselves!

The Past and Future of 3D

The story of 3D printing starts with the **invention** of the inkjet printer in 1976. Inkjet printers made it possible to print two-dimensional (2D), or flat, images on paper. Soon, people started thinking about printing 3D objects with other materials.

In 1984, Charles Hull invented a process for printing 3D objects. This process, called stereolithography, involved building 3D objects by putting thin layers of material on top of each other.

3D Systems still makes 3D printers today. These are parts for airplanes made with new technology from 3D Systems.

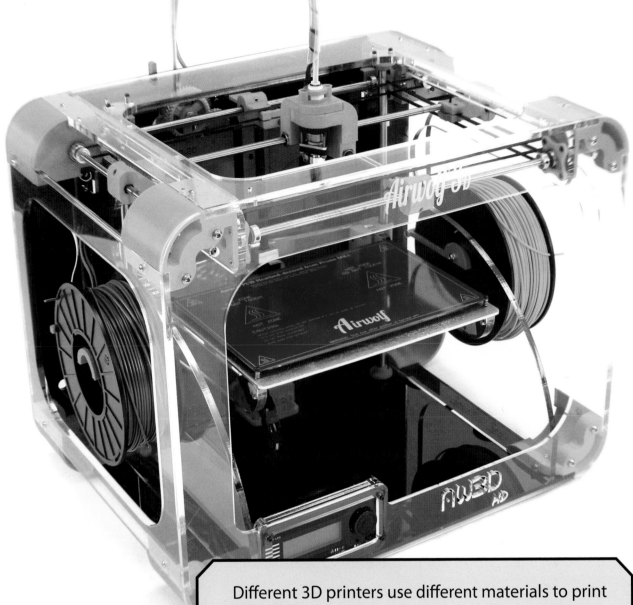

Different 3D printers use different materials to print things. Metal, glass, or plastic can all be used. This 3D printer uses spools of plastic.

Hull's company, 3D Systems, made the first machine that used stereolithography to print 3D objects in 1992. Since 1992, many other companies have made machines that can print 3D objects. In 1995, two students at the Massachusetts Institute of Technology came up with the term "3D printing."

Many people use 3D printers to make everyday objects like toys and jewelry, but 3D printers have many uses. Doctors can use 3D-printed bones to put inside of people. Some scientists make copies of dinosaur skeletons and ancient artifacts with 3D printers. This way, they can study these **fragile** objects without having to touch and possibly harm the originals. Parts for complex machines such as cars and airplanes can be created using 3D printing.

Prosthetics, or objects that take the place of missing body parts, can be made using 3D-printing technology.

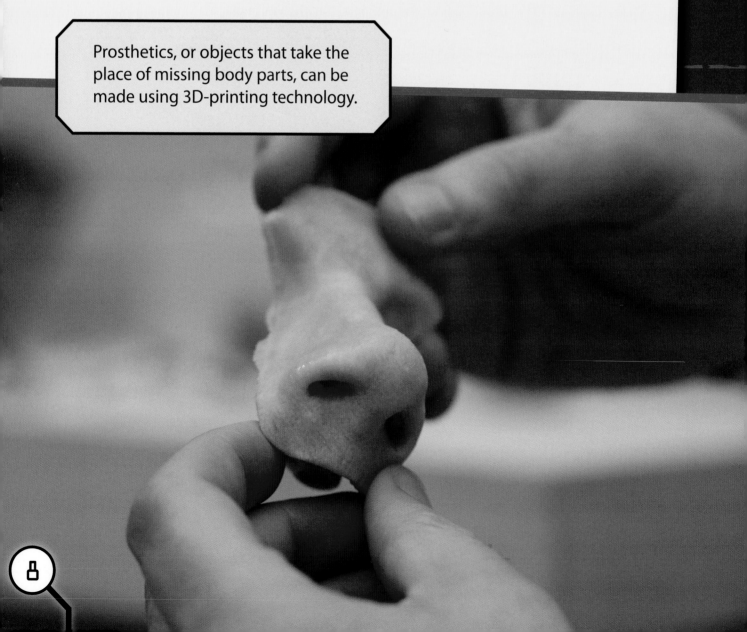

Even with all of these amazing uses for 3D printers, there is much more people want to do. Engineers are designing 3D printers that can print entire houses and buildings. Scientists and doctors are researching how to print working human organs like the liver and heart. With a little more time, who knows what 3D printers will be able to do?

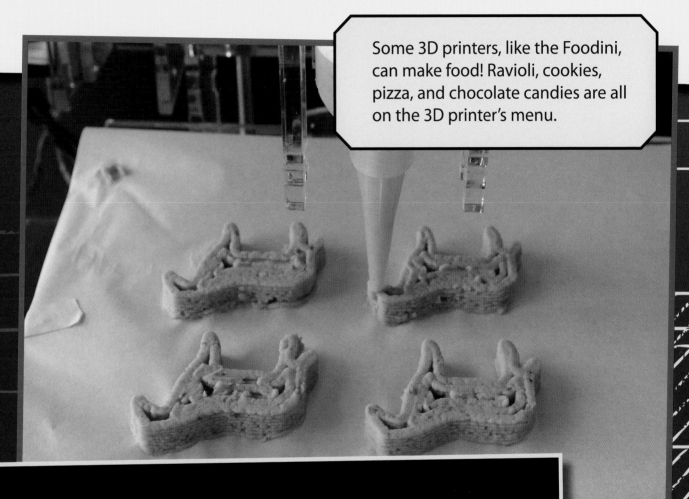

Some 3D printers, like the Foodini, can make food! Ravioli, cookies, pizza, and chocolate candies are all on the 3D printer's menu.

Printed Food

In the future, one of the most common types of printed materials may be food. In fact, Google, the tech company, has already served printed pasta in its cafeteria. NASA is even testing 3D printers that could make many different kinds of food for astronauts in space. One day, you might even eat your printed food with printed forks and knives on printed plates!

How Do 3D Printers Work?

To start a 3D-printing project, you must first make a digital 3D model of an object. You can do this using special computer software. Blender, 3DTin, and Autodesk's 123D programs are a few of the 3D-modeling programs that you can **download** or use on the Internet for free. These programs let you load a model and change it or build something new from scratch!

Another way to create a 3D model is to use a 3D scanner, such as the Microsoft Kinect or MakerBot Digitizer. Scanning is a quick and easy way to **upload** a model you can then edit.

Once you have finished a 3D model, it's time to print it! The 3D-modeling software will create a special file, which 3D printers use.

Working with 3D-modeling software can be tricky. Ask an adult to help you figure out how to work it.

With Ultimaker's Cura program, you can view, change the size of, and prepare your 3D model to be printed.

The special file you send to a 3D printer divides your 3D model into many layers called cross sections. The 3D printer prints each cross section by squeezing out a type of liquid material.

Building 3D Printers

All over the world, people are figuring out how to build their own 3D printers! Kodjo Afate Gnikou, an inventor in Togo, West Africa, built a 3D printer entirely from parts of other electronic devices that had been thrown away. He named his 3D printer W.AFATE. In the United States, Matthew Krueger made his own working 3D printer out of a LEGO Mindstorms kit, extra LEGO blocks, and a hot-glue gun.

Different 3D printers use different materials to print objects. Plastic, metal, glass, wax, and other materials can all be used. Plastic filament is the most common material used by home 3D printers.

Once a 3D printer has finished a layer, it prints the next layer on top of that one. It will keep doing this until the top layer has been printed and the object is done.

Most home 3D printers use plastic filament. There are many different kinds of plastic filaments that come in many different colors.

3D Printer Spaces

You can buy a 3D printer from many stores or websites that sell high-tech devices such as computers. However, a 3D printer is often more expensive than a brand-new computer.

Many adults are also involved in the maker movement. They are happy to teach kids what they know!

Online video tutorials, or lessons, can teach you many things you need to know about 3D printing. Have an adult help you find some.

If you do not have a 3D printer at home, do not worry! Many schools and public libraries are opening 3D printer spaces, where kids can learn how to use a 3D printer and make 3D objects. There might also be a makerspace in your town or city. Makerspaces are places where you can learn about all kinds of high-tech DIY projects, such as electronics, robotics, and 3D printing. One near you may even have a 3D printer that you can use for free or for a small fee.

MakerBot and the Thingiverse

MakerBot Industries is a 3D-printer company founded in Brooklyn, New York, in 2009. MakerBot makes easy-to-use consumer 3D printers and scanners. While some 3D printers are so expensive that only large companies can afford them, consumer 3D printers are cheaper. They are made for use in homes, schools, libraries, and small businesses.

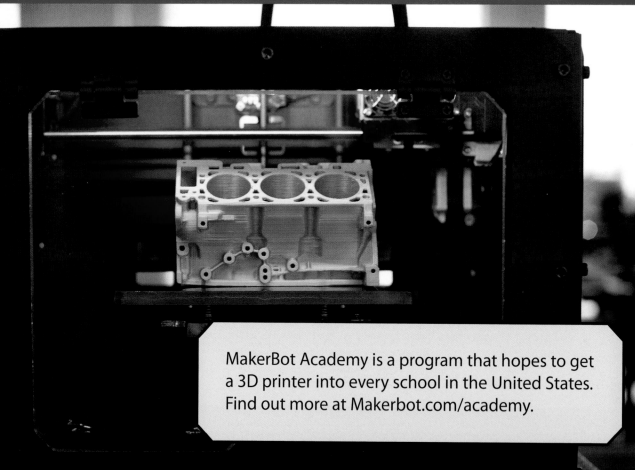

MakerBot Academy is a program that hopes to get a 3D printer into every school in the United States. Find out more at Makerbot.com/academy.

MakerBot Replicator™ 2X

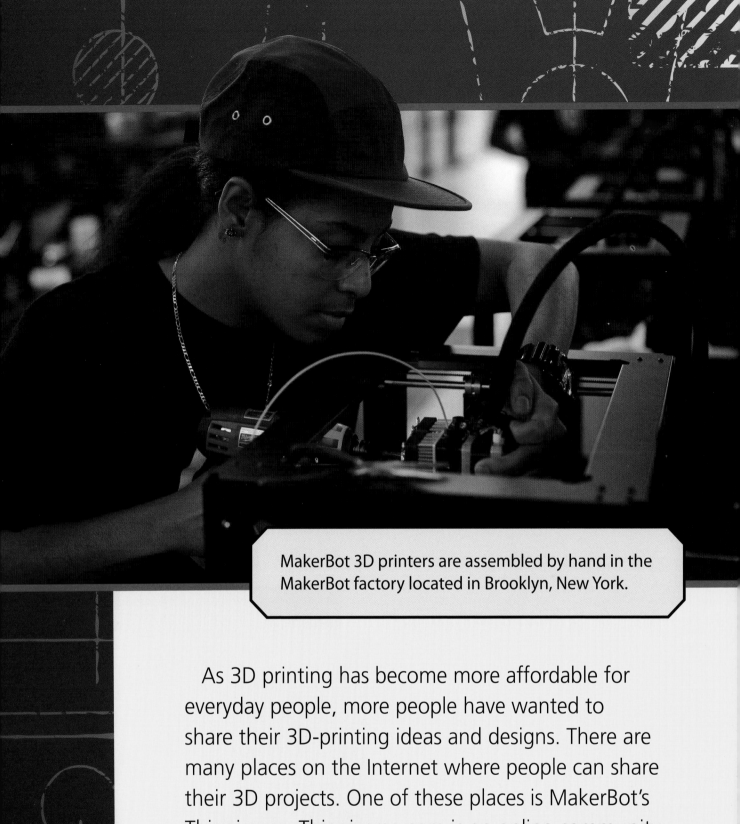

MakerBot 3D printers are assembled by hand in the MakerBot factory located in Brooklyn, New York.

As 3D printing has become more affordable for everyday people, more people have wanted to share their 3D-printing ideas and designs. There are many places on the Internet where people can share their 3D projects. One of these places is MakerBot's Thingiverse. Thingiverse.com is an online community where people can post their 3D projects, ask for advice, and look for new project ideas.

Mini Project: Jumping Frog

Some 3D projects can take a long time, but others are very quick to complete. A fun, quick project to try is the jumping frog from Thingiverse.

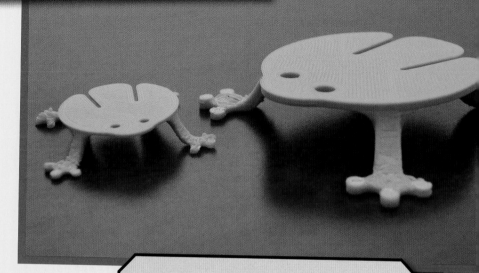

1) Go to Thingiverse.com /thing:268704 and download the model from the Thing Files tab.

2) Print the jumping frog.

3) Have an adult help you clip off the leg stands.

4) To make the jumping frog jump, just stand it up, press down on the tab, and then let your finger slip off the tab.

You will need:
- A computer
- Access to the Internet
- A 3D printer
- A pair of scissors

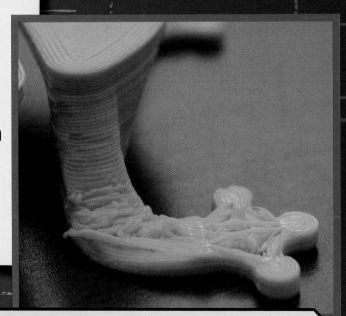

Sometimes, 3D projects don't come out the way you want them to. If that happens, make some adjustments and try again.

Most 3D printers can print only one color of filament at a time. Many people paint their 3D projects to make them look exactly how they want.

Choosing a Project

If you are new to 3D printing, you might want to try a project with easy-to-follow instructions. The MakerBot Thingiverse is full of easy 3D-printing projects. You can also find 3D-printing projects at Instructables.com, a website with step-by-step instructions and video **tutorials** for thousands of DIY projects. *Make* magazine's website, Makezine.com, also features many 3D-printing projects.

If you're up to the challenge, try building a model from scratch. You can base it on something you already have.

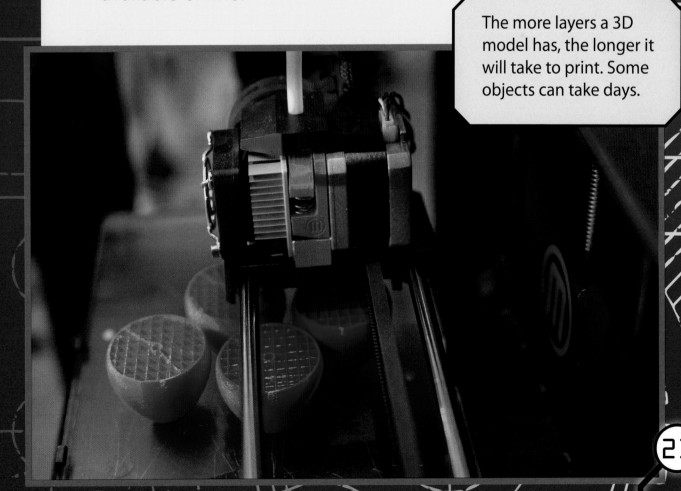

If you lose a game piece, you can print a new one with a 3D printer.

If you want to make your own design, change a design you downloaded, or print something at home, you will need to use a computer with 3D-modeling software. Free modeling software, such as Blender and Autodesk's 123D programs, are available online.

The more layers a 3D model has, the longer it will take to print. Some objects can take days.

To print your design, you need access to a 3D printer. If you do not have a 3D printer at home, check to see if there is a 3D-printer space in your school or public library. Your city or town may also have a makerspace with a 3D printer that you can use.

You can 3D print anything, even things to wear. Masks, shoes, dresses, and jewelry have all been 3D printed.

Filabot

If you use a 3D printer at home, you will need filament. The more you print, the more filament you will need. This can become expensive. Filabot systems make filament from pellets, or beads, of plastic very cheaply. Filabot.com sells filament and Filabot machines if people want to make their own filament at home. You and an adult can even build your own Filabot with the instructions found at Bit.ly/OTBAaC.

Waiting for your 3D object to come in the mail will be hard, but getting it will be very fun.

If you cannot find a 3D printer to use nearby, you can send your digital model to an online printing service such as Shapeways.com. For a fee, they will print your design and mail it to you. Makexyz.com lists people near you who have 3D printers. They are willing to print your project for a fee. Some of them will even help you with your design.

Make a Keychain with Your Name!

Autodesk's Tinkercad is great for your first 3D-printing project. You don't even have to download anything. It runs right on the Internet! You can make almost anything with Tinkercad and a little patience. For now, try making a keychain with your name on it.

You will need:

- A computer
- Access to the Internet
- Google Chrome 10 or newer or Mozilla Firefox 4 or newer

1

Go to Tinkercad.com and open the editor. You do not have to make an account. If you want an account, though, you must ask an adult to help you.

2

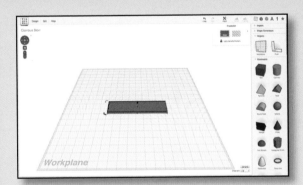

Drag a box onto the workplane. Make it thin by clicking the little white square on top and dragging it down. Next, make it into a rectangle by clicking on the little white box at a corner and dragging it.

Scroll down on the side menu to Holes and drag a cylinder hole onto the end of the rectangle.

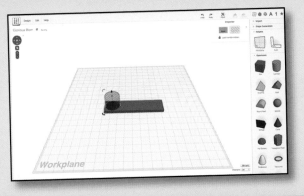

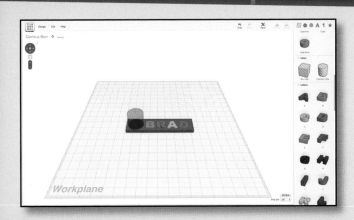

Scroll down on the side menu to Letters and pull letters onto the rectangle to spell your name. Change how tall and how big each letter is by clicking and dragging the little boxes on each letter when it is selected.

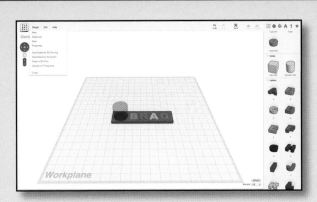

Once everything is how you want it, click on Design at the top left. You can save, download for 3D printing, order a 3D print, and more.

You can print the same project many times. Try printing it using different colors.

More Fun Projects

The Internet is full of easy 3D-printing projects for you to try! The next paragraphs describe some fun projects. Links to each of them can be found in the Projects Links box at the end of this chapter.

Many people use 3D printers to make things that don't have real uses. They just want to experiment or like how their design looks.

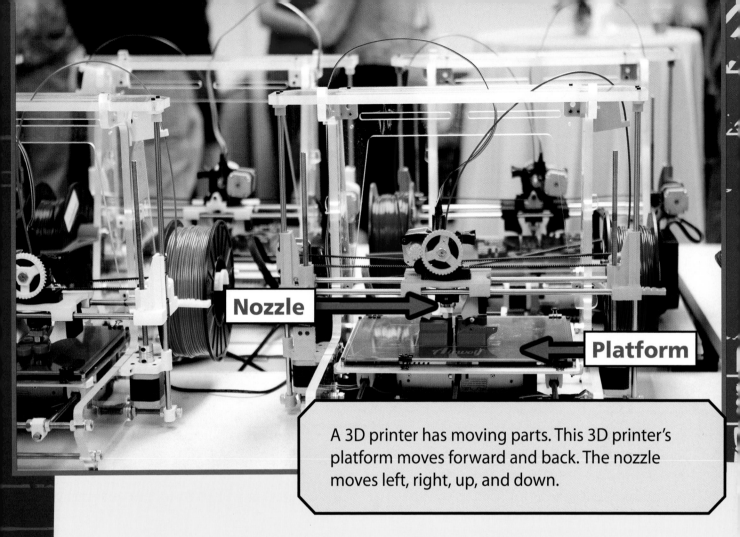

Nozzle

Platform

A 3D printer has moving parts. This 3D printer's platform moves forward and back. The nozzle moves left, right, up, and down.

You can make almost anything with a 3D printer. You can even turn yourself into a piece of art. One project online shows you how to make a 3D model of your head.

The following projects are fun and useful in everyday life. You can use the grooved teeth of a 3D-printed shark to hold a potato chip bag closed. The toothpaste pusher animal helps you squeeze out the last bits of toothpaste in your tube. The finger fork is a small flexible fork that fits around your fingertip!

Projects Links

3D Head - Makezine.com/projects/Print-Your-Head-in-3D
Shark Clip - Thingiverse.com/thing:14702
Toothpaste Pusher - Thingiverse.com/thing:49263
Finger Fork - Thingiverse.com/thing:112353

Make Your Idea Real!

DIY projects help you think creatively! Do you have ideas for cool inventions? What do you want to make? How can you make it happen? When you experiment with high-tech projects such as building robots or 3D printing, you are taking part in the maker movement!

If you aren't sure what to make, look at what others have made. It can help you figure out something you may want to print.

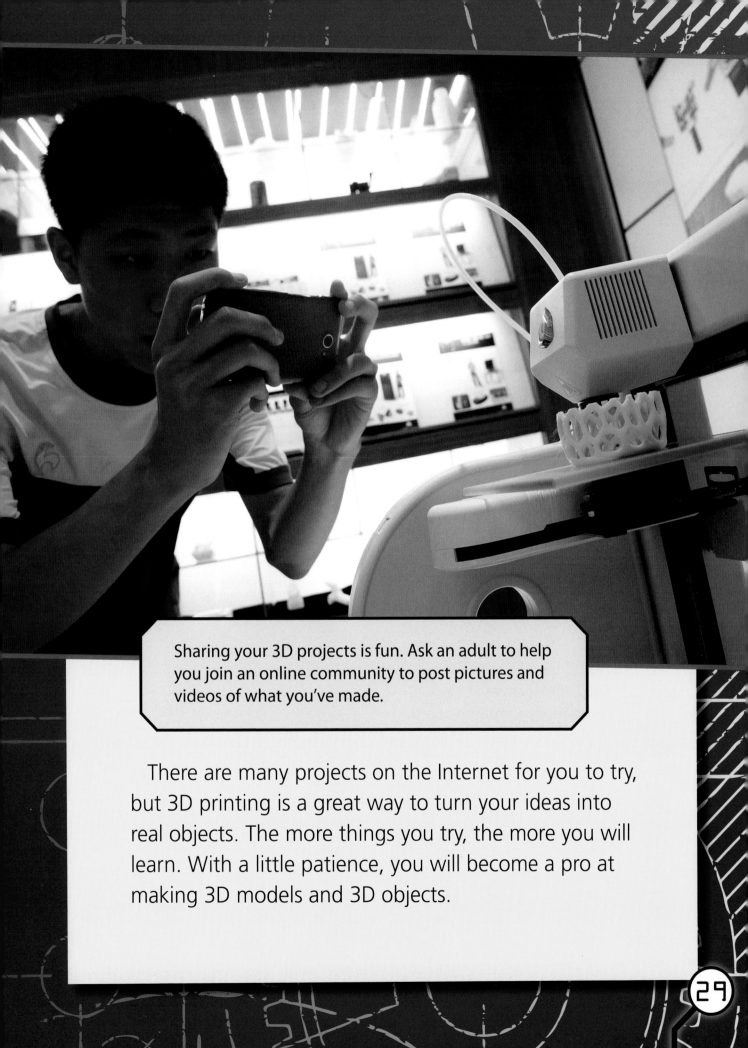

Sharing your 3D projects is fun. Ask an adult to help you join an online community to post pictures and videos of what you've made.

There are many projects on the Internet for you to try, but 3D printing is a great way to turn your ideas into real objects. The more things you try, the more you will learn. With a little patience, you will become a pro at making 3D models and 3D objects.

More About Making

Check out the lists below for more ways to learn about 3D printing. You can also ask an adult to help you use the library and search the Internet for other projects, books, and places to buy supplies!

Books

Diana, Carla. *Leo the Maker Prince: Journeys in 3D Printing.* Sebastopol, CA. Maker Media, Inc., 2013.

France, Anna Kaziunas. *Make: 3D Printing: The Essential Guide to 3D Printers.* Sebastopol, CA. Maker Media, Inc., 2013.

Websites

For projects and help, visit MakerBot's Thingiverse at Thingiverse.com. For 3D-printing projects, take a look at Instructables.com.

Free 3D-Modeling Software

The Autodesk 123D programs – 123dapp.com
FreeCAD - Freecadweb.org
SketchUp Make - Sketchup.com

Printers and Supplies

Airwolf3d.com
Ultimaker.com
Cubify.com
Makerbot.com

Glossary

artifacts (AR-tih-fakts) Objects created by humans from a past time.

digital model (DIH-juh-tul MAH-del) A representation of something made with and displayed on a computer.

download (DOWN-lohd) To copy data from one computer system to another or to a disk.

fragile (FRA-jul) Easily broken.

invention (in-VENT-shun) A new thing made by people.

replicas (REH-plih-kuz) Copies.

three-dimensional (THREE-deh-MENCH-nul) Having height, width, and depth. A flat picture, such as a photograph, is two-dimensional. A sculpture is three-dimensional.

tutorials (too-TOR-ee-ulz) Lessons.

upload (up-LOHD) To move data from one computer to another computer or disk.

Index

A
artifacts, 4, 8

B
Blender, 10, 21

C
company, 7, 9, 16
computer(s), 4, 14, 21, 24
copies, 4, 8

D
digital model, 4, 23

I
invention(s), 6, 28

L
layer(s), 6, 12–13

M
machine(s), 4, 7–8
maker movement, 5, 28
Massachusetts Institute of Technology, 7
material(s), 6, 9, 12–13

O
object(s), 4, 6–8, 10, 13, 15, 29

P
paper, 6

part(s), 4–5, 8, 12, 28
printer(s), 4–6, 8–10, 12–16, 18, 22–23, 27, 30
process, 6

S
scanning, 10
space stations, 4
stereolithography, 6–7
students, 7

T
3D Systems, 7, 30
toys, 4, 8
tutorials, 20

Websites

Due to the changing nature of Internet links, PowerKids Press has developed an online list of websites related to the subject of this book. This site is updated regularly. Please use this link to access the list:
www.powerkidslinks.com/maker/3dpr/